NEW ZEALAND
Bays and Beaches

NEW ZEALAND
Bays and Beaches

NZ
Visitor
Publications
Ltd.
Auckland
New Zealand

Stretches of New Zealand coastline

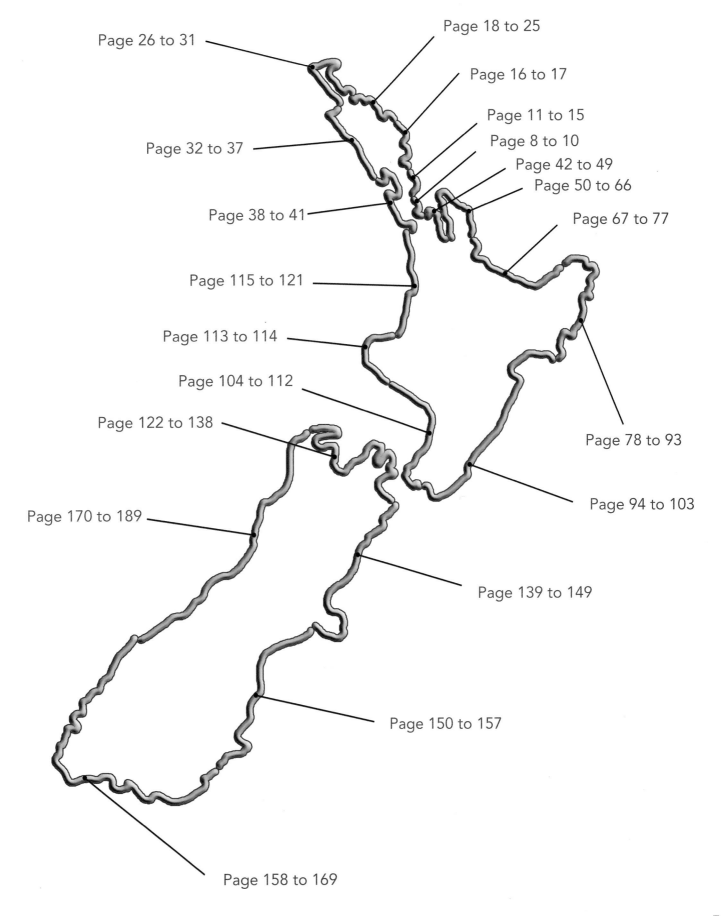

New Zealand with its two main islands, the North Island and South Island surrounded by ocean, has almost 17,000 km of coastline. This is reason enough to devote a book just to its bays and beaches. You can see many types of coastal landscape in New Zealand – from snow-white, golden or black sandy beaches to steep rocky coasts – suitable for a great variety of water sports. The coast can change appearance within a few kilometres with the most beautiful and idyllic beaches not necessarily found along the main tourist routes. In this book we also take you off to the remotest beaches and bays around the two main islands.

Our virtual tour begins in Auckland, the largest city in New Zealand, surrounded by many glorious bays. From there we continue along the east coast of the Northland region, through the Bay of Islands, across the top of the North Island and back down the west coast to Auckland. The Northland region with its temperate to subtropical climate is one of the most popular holiday areas in New Zealand. Its strongly indented coastline was formed after the last ice age when many mainland river valleys flooded as water levels rose. Prolifically branched estuaries were formed on the west coast while broad harbours with numerous islands emerged on the east coast. South of Auckland we continue along the Seabird Coast, the west coast of the Firth of Thames, to Coromandel Peninsula. We travel around the forested peninsula with its jagged coastline and numerous small bays with magnificent sandy beaches and follow the Bay of Plenty coastline to the eastern tip of East Cape. This area remains one of New Zealand tourism's best kept secrets. The trip along the coast offers spectacular scenery with golden sandy beaches interspersed with jagged, stony bays rimmed with bush and Pohutukawa trees – a paradise for anglers and water sport enthusiasts. Once around the eastern tip we will show you the Hawke's Bay coastline and continue in a southward direction to Cape Palliser, the southern tip of the North Island. There we visit the local beaches of Wellington, the capital, and proceed northwards along the Tasman coast. We arrive first at expansive sand dune landscapes before reaching the surf coast around Mount Egmont, known as a surfer's paradise. The west coast between Mt Egmont and Auckland is mostly very rocky and is only partly accessible.

On returning to Auckland we leap over to the South Island, starting our tour on the northern tip of Farewell Spit. We guide you to the idyllic beaches of Abel Tasman National Park, through the unique landscape of the Marlborough Sounds and from Picton, over Underwood Road along the coast to Blenheim. The coastline from Blenheim to Kaikoura is mostly very rugged and rocky. There are only a few small bays along the east coast to Christchurch, however, the Banks Peninsula features some idyllic bays and many water sporting opportunities. The southernmost part of the South Island features stunning beaches along the Southern Scenic Route although the climate here is rather harsh. The bays and fiords in Fiordland National Park, the south-western tip of the South Island can only be reached by boat. And finally we show you the west coast of the South Island with its deserted, wild, romantic landscape. A mere 35,000 people live along the 600 km stretch of coastline, one of New Zealand's tourist highlights stretching west of the Southern Alps and graduating from giant rain forests to breathtaking coastal scenery.

Above and below:

Auckland's Waitemata Harbour probably has the highest density of boats of any area in New Zealand. The natural harbour opens from Stanley Bay into the Hauraki Gulf and possesses a number of small inlets which serve the water sporting needs of residents and visitors to Auckland. Some of these can be seen on this and the following double page. A number of tidal rivers such as the Henderson River and Whau Creek empty into the harbour.

The Harbour Bridge spans the Waitemata Harbour. The first regular transport across the harbour goes back to the late 19th Century when a ferry service was established to connect the isolated North Shore districts with the city. The idea of building a bridge to cope with rising traffic was born already in 1929. For some time a tunnel was also considered but this idea was subsequently abandoned. It took 30 years to reach an agreement on building a bridge and thus the present bridge did not finally start operation until 1959.

Right:
The Port of Auckland, New Zealand's largest freight harbour is visited annually by more than 1,700 freight ships. Some 5.5 million tonnes of freight pass through the harbour every year with 60 percent of the country's freight business transpiring here.

Remaining pictures of this page:
Various views of the Waitemata Harbour.

Bays in Waitemata Harbour.

Rangitoto Island as seen from Mission Bay.

Okauhu Bay.

Mission Bay.

St Heliers Bay.

The town of Whangaparaoa on the peninsula of the same name was Auckland's first holiday region and has developed into an upmarket residential area which today consists of Arkles Bay, Red Beach, Stanmore Bay, Little Manly, Big Manly, Tindalls Beach, Gulf Harbour and Whangaparaoa. On this page you can see just a few of the beautiful bays located on this peninsula whose Maori name means ‚whale bay'.

Top:
Matakatia Bay lies between Little Manly and Hobbs Bay on the southern side of the peninsula.

Second picture from above:
Army Bay, part of Red Beach. The red-coloured sand stems from a red shell which has been
swept up on the beach for thousands of years and ground to sand.

Right:
Tindalls Bay on the north coast of the peninsula, east of Big Manly Beach.

Above, second row, left and right:
The elongated Stanmore Bay stretches from Tarihunga Point in the south-east to Red Beach in the north-east.

. *Double page 12/13 and pages 14 and 15:*

Orewa Beach. The magnificent sandy beach which runs the whole length of Orewa town is considered one of the most beautiful beaches in New Zealand and is a tempting spot for swimming and surfing. At the northern end of the beach is the Alice Eaves Scenic Reserve. In 1859, Captain Isaac Rhodes Cooper from the 58th regiment acquired land here for a farm which today has become Orewa.

The Kowhai Coast, a particularly attractive stretch of coastal landscape stretches from Wenderholm near Waiwera in the south to Pakiri Beach in the north and is a paradise for water sport enthusiasts. More than 26 beaches on the Kowhai Coast and eight islands which lie off the coast in the Hauraki Gulf offer excellent possibilities for boating, fishing, diving and swimming. The coast is named after the many kowhai trees growing here.

Top left and right:
View of Kawau Bay and Kawau Island loved by fishermen.

Right column, second picture from above:
Omaha Beach near Leigh.

Right column, third picture from above:
Mangawhai Harbour at the northern end of the Kowhai Coast.

Right:
Snells Beach in Kawau Bay.

Right:
Stretch of coast near Leigh.

Right:
Urquarts Bay in Whangarei Harbour.

Right:
Pataua River joining Ngunguru Bay.

Right:
Ocean Beach at Bream Head, a promontory with 495 metre high cliffs marking the end of Whangarei Harbour and the northernmost point of Bream Bay; off shore are the Hen and Chicken Islands.

Right:
Sandy Bay is a large, sandy bay composed of many small bays such as Woolleys Bay, Whale Bay, Sheltered Bay and Oruaea Bay. Steep hills form the backdrop. A paradise for hikers, water sporting enthusiasts and anglers.

Left:
Teal Bay a cove in Helena Bay.

Left:
Pomare Bay.

Left:
Waikere Inlet.

Left and below:
The very attractive Waipiro Bay with its cliffs.

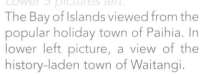

Lower 3 pictures left:
The Bay of Islands viewed from the popular holiday town of Paihia. In lower left picture, a view of the history-laden town of Waitangi.

Double page 18/19:
One of the first settlers here named the place and the idyllic bay after his wife, Helena.

Right und page 20 second picture from above:
Orongo bay in the Pomare Bay, a southern extension of the Bay of Islands. The Bay of Islands is a large, very many-fingered bay on the east coast of the Northland peninsula, a system of drowned river valleys created when they were flooded by the sea.
.

Right bottom and double page 22/23:
Impressions of Russell, the centre of the Bay of Islands. Right, Russell's Long Beach.

Left and below:
Whangaroa Harbour is situated about 6 km off State Highway 10 and is a meeting spot for sport fishermen who embark on deep sea fishing trips from here.

Two pictures above:

Mangonui Harbour was formerly an important harbour for trading ships and a processing centre for kauri wood. Today the emphasis is on deep sea fishing and all varieties of water sports. The harbour opens up into Doubtless Bay, a broad bay on the northern Pacific Coast of the Far North District; Knuckle Point on Karikari Peninsula in the north-west and Berghan Point on the south-east side describe its two end points.

Above:

From 1902 to 1912 an underwater cable to Australia terminated in Cable Bay, thus the name.

Below:

Taipa Bay according to Maori history, was the bay in which Kupe the legendary Polynesian seaman set foot on New Zealand soil in 950 A.D.

Page 25:
Kerikeri, centre of citrus fruit in New Zealand, is nestled on Kerikeri Inlet, an estuary which opens into the Bay of Islands in the east. Pictured above, the Stone Store, New Zealand's oldest stone building.

Left:
Cape Maria van Diemen on the southern end of Te Werahi Beach.

Right:
The Cape Reinga lighthouse.

Cape Reinga on the northernmost tip of the Aupouri Peninsula which forms the northernmost part of the North Island of New Zealand. The peninsula consists almost entirely of sand which in the course of time has collected there and hardened. Aupouri is the name of the local Maori tribe and was originally the name of the canoe on which their forefathers arrived in New Zealand in 900 A.D.

The best known lighthouse in New Zealand stands on Cape Reinga which rises a step 290 m above sea level. Below is the point where the Tasman Sea and the Pacific Ocean meet. The two masses of water crashing into one another form what is called the Columbia bank Maelstrom with waves which can reach a height of 10 m in stormy weather. The treacherous sea off Cape Reinga has thus been the cause of numerous boating disasters in the past. There is a wonderful view to be had from the cape which reaches from Cape Maria van Diemen in the west to North Cape in the east. In clear weather you can make out the Three Kings Islands off the coast.

Double page 28/29:
Ninety Mile Beach is a long stretch of sand with sand dunes backing onto bush, which extends along the western side of the Aupouri Peninsula. It stretches from Ahipara Bay in the south to Scott Point in the north. The beach is officially designated a road, however, numerous car wrecks bear witness to the danger of getting stuck in the sand and being overwhelmed by an incoming tide which may rise as much a s 3.8 m within six hours. As the region does not have a lot more to offer visitors than its well-known beach, people have come up with ideas to get their share of the tourism pie. Bus tours as well as four-wheel drive trips are offered along the beach. You can also ride or drive over the sand in a so-called quad bike. In addition, the almost endless beach and giant dunes offer opportunities for extensive beach hikes, fishing, shell collecting, surfing, sunbathing and kite flying. Those looking for sport and adventure can try dune riding, body boarding or hang gliding. The latest for adventure sport enthusiasts is Blokarting in which you speed over the sand in sand yachts or Blokarts which weigh a mere 25 kg. Every year in February fishermen from all over the world meet at Ninety Mile Beach to take part in the Surf-casting Snapper Fishing Contest. More than 1,000 fishermen compete to snag the fattest snapper and the prize money of NZ$75,000 which it yields. It is also from here that the protected migratory seabirds, godwits and knots set off on their annual journey to Siberia and Alaska in March having spent the summer months in the north of New Zealand and other islands of the west Pacific. Occasionally you can see blue penguins on the beach or wild horses grazing on patches of grass near the water.

The name ‚Ninety Mile Beach' is incorrect or at least exaggerated as the beach is only 52 miles long (84 km) from Shipwreck Bay at Ahipara to Kahokawa Beach just below Scott Point, or a maximum of 60 miles (96 km) when measured all the way to Cape Maria van Diemen.

The land beyond the beach used to be covered by extensive kauri forests, today the Aupouri Forest extends over about two thirds of Ninety Mile Beach down to the water proximity.

Double page 30/31:
Ahipara Bay – the southernmost part of Ninety Mile Beach.

Top and above:
View from Opononi on the Hokianga Harbour and the sand dunes of North Head.

Below:
The Hokianga Harbour is a long fiord-like harbour on the west coast of the North Auckland peninsula. The natural harbour extends 30 km from the coast in a north-easterly, inland direction to Kohukohu where it branches into two estuaries from the Mangamuka and Waihou Rivers. From the banks rise steep, forested hills. Hokianga Harbour is a system of sunken river valleys which used to be referred to as the Hokianga River. North Head, a promontory at the entrance to the harbour, consists of cliffs and shifting dunes some of which reach a height of 170 m. On the southern coastline of the Hokianga Harbour there are beautiful white sandy beaches at the seaside resorts of Omapere and Opononi.

Page 33 and double pages 34/35 and 36/37:
Ripiro Ocean Beach at Baylys Beach. An almost untouched beach interspersed with shifting sand dunes stretching over an area almost 100 km long. The town Baylys Beach has become a popular holiday spot.

32

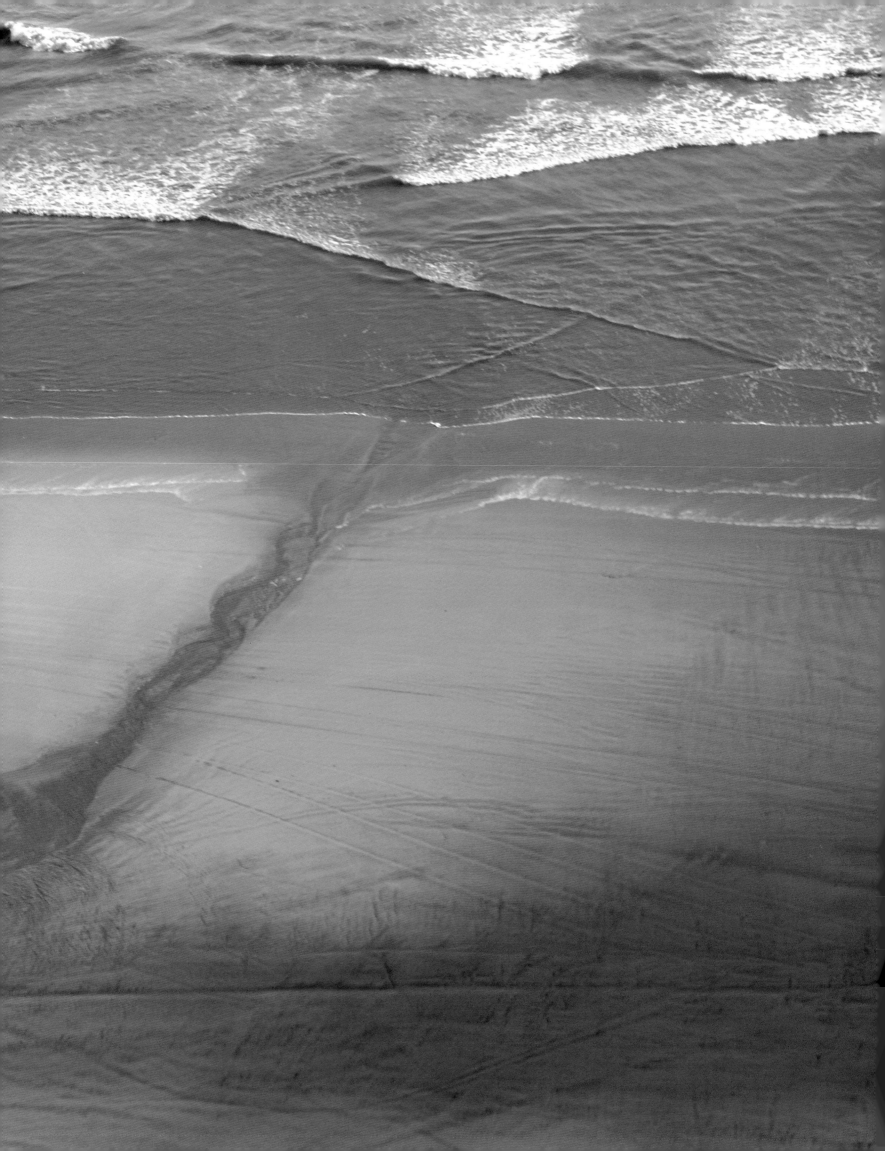

Top:
Pahi Beach, a small farming community at the tip of a headland between the Pahi and the Paparoa River, is popular with the locals for swimming.

Above:
Shellys Beach, a holiday settlement on the south-western coast of the Kaipara Harbour. This beautiful beach is popular for picnicking, swimming, fishing and boating.

Below:
Te Henga – Bethells Beach at the Waitakere River mouth.

Above:
Karekare Beach near Piha, on the eastern coast of Waitakere City.

Below:
Coastline at Titirangi on the Manukau Harbour. The Manukau Harbour is a large but relatively shallow natural harbour to the south of the Auckland isthmus which opens into the Tasman Sea through a narrow channel between Whatipu, Waitakere City in the north and South Head on the tip of the Awhitu Peninsula in the south. It covers an area of about 388 sq. km on the 386 km long coastline and was formed less than 10 million years ago as the sea flooded large portions of the North Island.

Double page 40/41:
Piha, a farming community and surf beach at the western foot of the Waitakere Ranges on the west coast of Waitakere City.
The powerful surf makes Piha one of the best known surf beaches in New Zealand but it also harbours dangers for swimmers and surfers. In the summer months, it is a meeting point for the many surfers who participate in surfing competitions which are often accompanied by beach parties and live concerts. At the mouth of the Piha Stream is a large projection called Lion Rock. If you attempt the steep, 101 m climb to the top you will be rewarded with a magnificent view.

Above and left:
Halfmoon Bay near Howick

Below:
Swimming beach in the Howick city district

Above:
Beachlands beach.

Right:
Omana Beach.

Below:
Umupuia Beach (or Duders Beach) at Umupuia.

Double page 44/45:
Cockle Bay in the south-east of Howick.

Double page 46/47:
Umupuia or Duders Beach on the Maraetai Coast Road.

Left:
Waikawa Bay on the Clevedon coast.

Left:
Kawakawa Bay on the southern coastline of the Tamaki Strait. Given the very slight slope of the coast the beach is well suited for children and those with limited swimming skills. Kawakawa Bay is also known as Ruakawakawa.

Left:
Coast by Orere Point a small beach settlement on the Orere headland on the north-western coast of the Firth of Thames.

Left:
Matingarahi Point, approx. 10 km south-east of Orere Point.

All pictures on this page:
The Seabird Coast near Miranda. The area features thermal pools with the largest hot water pool in New Zealand. Another special feature of Miranda is the bird sanctuary located nearby with 8,500 ha. of mudflats inhabited by a multitude of sea birds including many arctic migratory birds. The abundance of worms and crustaceans in the mud flat region form the basis of the birds' diet.

The forested Coromandel Peninsula separates the western part of the Bay of Plenty from the Hauraki Gulf and the Firth of Thames and encompasses the mainland and islands north of the Hauraki Plains and south of Great Barrier Island. The peninsula's landscape whose backbone is formed by the Coromandel Ranges is characterized by steep rocky cliffs, deep gorges, many babbling brooks and rivers and a jagged coastline. The landscape was formed between 2 and 20 million years ago in the late Tertiary by volcanic activity which covered considerably older layers (up to 40 million years old) of limestone, coal and greywacke interspersed with granite. Within the last 2-3 million years vertical land movements along nearby fault lines have led to the formation of the Hauraki Plains/Firth of Thames region which is bordered in the east by the Coromandel Ranges and in the west by the Hunua Ranges, and this has partially uncovered these older layers of stone. In the course of time the highland was eroded by the passage of water through it and the cliffs of the coastline made steeper by the sea, especially on the eastern side.

The richly forested mountain regions and numerous bays and beaches of the Coromandel Peninsula attract tourists interested in both hiking and water sports. The warmer climate here, with temperatures of around 30 °C in summer and 11 °C in winter contribute to making the peninsula one of the most popular holiday regions in New Zealand. Numerous interesting sights including many historical sites from the days of gold digging and kauri felling make a visit worthwhile. It is also possible to explore the gorgeous landscape by horse or mountain bike. Contributing to Coromandel's special flair are the many artists and crafts people who live here; you can visit their workshops and shops along the Coromandel Craft Trail.

If you follow the west coast of the Coromandel Peninsula northward from Coromandel township you will pass numerous bays lined by grand old Pohutukawa trees which are covered in bright red flowers around Christmas time. This stretch of coast offers an array of breathtaking views of the coast and nearby islands.

Above:
The Coromandel Harbour.

This page and double page 52/53:
Waikawau Bay on the southern side of the Waikawau River on the northern tip of the eastern Coromandel Peninsula. The bay with its beautiful sandy beach is good for swimming and fishing.

Left:
Little Bay.

Left:
Tuateawa Bay and Tuateawa
Point.

Left:
Whangapoua Harbour south of
the Whangapoua township.

Left:
In earlier times there was a fairly
large Maori settlement at Opito
Bay traces of which can still be
seen. The bay is perfect for all
kinds of water sports.

Right:
Otama Beach.

Right and below:
Matarangi Beach on Omaro Spit, a natural breakwater in front of Whangapoua Harbour.

Right:
Motuhua Point by Kuaotunu West with its beautiful white sandy beaches is situated on the northern side of the hilly peninsula between Mercury Bay and Whitianga Harbour in the south, and Whangapoua Harbour in the north.

Double page 56/57:
Mercury Bay, a natural harbour featuring a number of small islands reaches from the 127 m high Cook Bluff in the south to Opito Point in the north. The bay is the outer part of a flooded former valley with Whitianga Harbour forming its inner section.

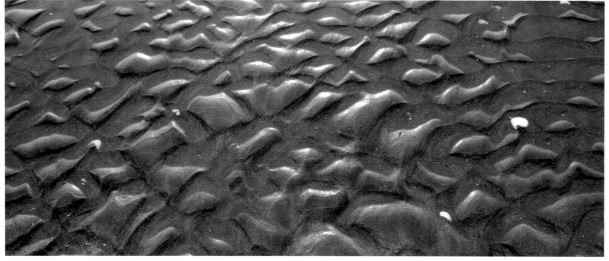

All pictures on this page:
Whitianga Harbour in Mercury Bay. A ferry connects the boat moorings in Whitianga to a landing on the opposite side of the Whitianga Harbour. The stone Kai ferry landing was built on 1837 for the kauri timber trade and is the oldest ferry landing in New Zealand. Whitianga was one of the first places in New Zealand in which Captain James Cook made a landing on his November 1769 journey.

Above:
Cooks Beach in Mercury Bay is marked by the lofty Shakespeare Cliffs in the west and the headland known as Cook Bluff in the east. The 3-km long beach covered in golden sand is especially popular with water sport enthusiasts. James Cook after whom the bay was named anchored here on November 5, 1769 in his ship "Endeavour". Together with the astronomer, Charles, he observed the flight of the planet Mercury through the sun's orbit in order to determine the length of the bay. Before Cook left the bay again he inscribed the date and name of his ship on one of the trees close to the water, hoisted the English flag and claimed the land in the name of King George III.

Below:
Somewhat south of the ferry landing is Flaxmill Bay at the eastern end of which the Shakespeare Cliffs can be found. The cliffs separate Cooks Beach from Flaxmill Bay. On their highest point is an outlook with a magnificent view of Mercury Bay and a monument dedicated to Captain Cook's landing. Cook also named the cliffs – their silhouette reminding him of Shakespeare's visage.

Right:
Hahei Beach.

Double page 60/61:
The glorious 1.5 km long Hahei Beach edged with Pohutukawa trees offers a fine selection of swimming, fishing and boating activities. In the Te Pare Point Historic Reserve located on Hereheretaura Point on the eastern end of the beach you can still see the terraces of an old Maori pa. The waters off the coast form the 9 km² Cathedral Cove Marine Reserve – Te Whanganui A Hei, which also includes a number of islands. Here, stony reefs, complex caves and stone arches create a multifarious undersea world – an excellent spot for snorkelling and diving.

Top and above:
Hot Water Beach on the east coast of the Coromandel Peninsula is one of the main attractions of the area due to its hot water springs. Thermal springs emerge from the sand right on the water's edge. You have about two hours either side of low tide to dig a thermal pool in which to enjoy mineral waters which can reach a temperature of up to 64 °C. However, swimming is not recommended at this beautiful beach as surf conditions can be dangerous.

Page 63:
You can only access Cathedral Cove by foot or by boat – it is a small bay but one of the greatest natural beauties on the Coromandel Peninsula.

Double page 64/65:
Hoho Rock in Cathedral Cove has been photographed many thousands of times and is widely known for its unique and beautiful form.

Tairua Harbour between Tairua and Pauanui, on the east coast of the Coromandel Peninsula. A passenger ferry connects the two townships on opposite sides of the harbour entrance. Tairua, like its twin township Pauanui, is a popular holiday destination where many affluent New Zealanders own a holiday home. A gorgeous sandy beach, clear water and a choice of places to moor boats offer optimal conditions for many kinds of water sport.

4-km long Whangamata Beach is ideal for surfing and windsurfing. There are excellent fishing grounds off the coast where amongst other things, crayfish are prolific. Whangamata marks the south-eastern end of the Coromandel Peninsula.

The elongated Bay of Plenty on the north coast of the North Island runs in a broad arch from the east coast of the Coromandel Peninsula eastwards to Cape Runaway, 50 km north-east of East Cape. Off the coast are a number of small islands at varying distances to the mainland. The Bay of Plenty is considered New Zealand's fruit – fertile volcanic soil and a sunny climate make for plentiful fruit harvests.

Moreover, the Bay of Plenty is one of the most favoured holiday regions in the North Island with its magnificent golden sandy beaches.

Top:
Maketu is a popular swimming beach with excellent surfing and good boating, fishing and swimming. The name which implies that the Arawa canoe from the "Great Fleet" landed here is still inhabited predominantly by descendants of the Arawa people.

Above:
Pukehina Beach, a stretch of sand on which New Zealanders traditionally built their simple baches, many of which have now become mundane beach houses.

Double page 68/69:
View of the Tauranga Harbour with Matakana Island off the coast.

Double page 70/71:
Omanu Beach at Mt Maunganui is part of the elongated Papamoa Beach.

Page 73:
View from Mt Maunganui of the like-named holiday town and the Tauranga Harbour.

Top:
Papamoa Beach. This kilometre-long beach is ideal for swimming and surfing. Papamoa Beach is also a popular target for amateur fishermen. One of the region's specialities is tuatua pipis (small shellfish) which you can collect off the beach at low tide.

Above:
Kohioawa Beach near Matata. The locals often come to this beach to fish for flounder, golden carp, whitebait and eels, or to collect pipis.

Below:
The Pukehina Beach between Maketu and Matata.

The mouth of the Whakatane River on the eastern side of which is Whakatane township. Some 50 km off the coast, White Island – a small, volcanic island whose highly active volcano is under constant observation – emerges from the water.

Left:
Ohope Beach, a 15-km long sandy beach which extends between Whakatane Heads and the entrance to Ohiwa Harbour.

Left:
Whitebaiting at the Whakatane River mouth.

Right:
Ohiwa Harbour near Whakatane, a long natural harbour separated from the Bay of Plenty by a lengthy narrow sandbank on the Pacific side of which is Ohope Beach. It encompasses an area of 2,700 ha with 86 kms of coastline. At low tide the water drops so far that about 70 percent of the harbour turns into sand banks and mud flats attracting a large variety of seabirds in search of food.

Right:
The beautiful sandy Waiotahi Beach near Opotiki.

Right:
Hikuwai Beach near Tirohanga.

Right:
The beach eventually ends at Whituare Bay near Opape and turns into rocky cliffs where a significant quantity of driftwood is washed up. Consequently the area is less suitable for swimming but makes for great fishing.

The eastern headland on New Zealand's North Island between Opotiki, East Cape, Gisborne and Wairoa is referred to as Eastland. Despite the sunny climate and the wonderful landscape, Eastland is still one of the spots in New Zealand relatively undiscovered by tourists. The drive along the coast offers spectacular scenery composed of golden sandy beaches interspersed with jagged rocky bays lined by bush and Pohutukawa trees.

Left:
Omaio Bay, a sheltered bay ideal for surfing and swimming.

Left:
Hariki Beach by Te Kaha.

Left:
The coast off Te Kaha.

Right:
Maraetai Bay and Wharekura Point, glorious bays and beaches in the direct vicinity of Te Kaha, a popular holiday spot.

Right:
Whanarua Bay is one of the most beautiful beaches along the eastern Bay of Plenty.

Right:
Papatea Bay.

Bottom:
Waihau Bay, with its rocky shores is not far from Cape Runaway a headland which marks the north-eastern end of the Bay of Plenty. Captain James Cook named the cape during his first journey after an event on October 31 1769. As five Maori war canoes approached he ordered shots to be aimed over their heads. The Maori attackers turned tail and Cook named the cape after their "runaway".

Double page 80/81:
The magnificent remote Hicks Bay extends in a south-eastward direction to Haupara Point.

Above and left:
Punaruku Beach near Te Araroa, west of the mouth of the Waitere River on the shores of Kawakawa Bay. The coast between here and East Cape was formerly the scene of many a shipping disaster. Today the elongated rocky platforms which are revealed at low tide attract geologists, divers and fishermen.

Page 83 and double page 84/85:
On the 25-km trip from Te Araroa to East Cape there are sand and pebble beaches as well as some unique rock formations the likes of which can be seen nowhere else in New Zealand.

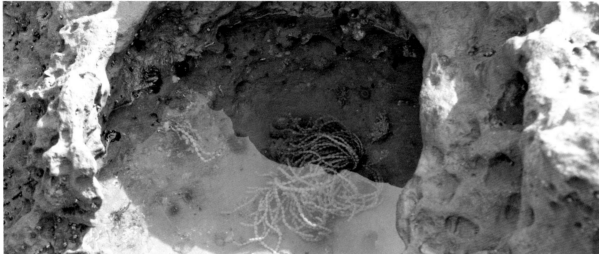

All pictures on this page:
Interesting rock formations at Horoera Point between Te Aroha and East Cape.

A steep path including 686 steps leads to the summit of Opotiki Hill where East Cape lighthouse stands majestically, 140 km above sea level. Its light marks the easternmost point of the New Zealand mainland. Just off the cape is East Island where the lighthouse originally stood. However, it was very difficult to land on the small island with not so much as a beach and slipping cliffs threatened the lighthouse keeper's dwellings. In 1906, after four men had been drowned in the attempt to deliver supplies to the island, the warning system was transferred to its present position. It is the easternmost lighthouse in the world. The light, housed in a 14 m high tower, flashes every ten seconds and can be seen from a distance of 48 km. Like all New Zealand lighthouses, this one on East Cape is now unmanned and controlled from Wellington. The steep climb up the hill is rewarded with a magnificent panorama and it is a wonderful place from which to watch the sun rise.

Above:
At the beginning of the 20th Century the largest settlement on the east coast and administrative centre for the region was located in the very attractive landscape of Waipiro Bay. The bay which was formerly called Oben Bay was an important port of call on coastal shipping voyages. Today, the once bustling township of Waipiro Bay is more reminiscent of a ghost town.

Below and page 89 top:
Tokomaru Bay with its impressive cliffs forms an attractive landscape while offering good fishing and surfing. The harbour at Waima on the northern end of the bay is now used for commercial fishing.

Above and right:
You can get to Anarau Bay with its beautiful golden sands a few kilometres south of The Three Bridges by back road. Captain Cook visited the bay in October 1769, his visit being commemorated by a plaque and an obelisk at the mouth of the Hawai River. In the bay lays Motuoroi Island.

Double page 90/91:
Tolaga Bay has an excellent beach for swimming and the longest jetty in New Zealand at 660 m. It was built between 1926 and 1929 and enabled freight ships to land on any tide. Before road connections were built all essential goods were delivered to the bay by sea and the region's trading goods also carried by ship. In 1967 the pier was closed to shipping traffic.

Left:
Pariokonohi Point with its marine reserve Te Tapuwae O Rongokako.

Left:
The coast at Tatapouri which mainly consists of rocky reefs.

Left:
There is a beautiful stretch of sand and rock pools at Makorori Beach.

Left:
Okito Beach.

Page 93 top and bottom:
The golden sandy beach at Waikanae.

The triangular, hilly Mahia Peninsula extends southwards from the north-eastern end of Hawke Bay. The coast of the peninsula is characterized by long, golden sandy beaches and interesting rock formations making it a popular holiday destination.

Top:
View of the peninsula.

Above and below:
Oraka Beach on the northern side of the Mahia Peninsula.

Above:
Mahia Beach.

Below:
Moemoto Beach.

Double page 96/97:
Waitaniwha Bay.

Double page 98/99:
Hawke Bay near Clifton. Some 10 km south-east of Clifton on the southern end of Hawke Bay lies Cape Kidnappers where you will find the only mainland gannet colony in the world. From October to March you can observe 10,000 gannets in the bird sanctuary tending their offspring.

Double page 100/101:
Waimarama Beach lies opposite the bleak cliffs of Bare Island. This wonderful beach is ideal for surfing.

Left:
Ocean Beach lies approx. midway along this long stretch of sand which extends from the southern side of Cape Kidnappers to Waimarama Beach.

Left:
The stony beach at Marine Parade in Napier.

Left:
White Rock, a reef which projects from the mouth of the Whawanui River into the sea.

At Cape Palliser on the southern end of the Aorangi mountains, an 18 m high lighthouse stands on a hill 70 m above sea level – it is the only lighthouse in New Zealand painted red and white. The cape was named on February 7, 1770 by Captain Cook after his friend Sir Hugh Palliser, following his first circumnavigation of the North Island. The Cape Palliser lighthouse started operation on October 27, 1987 and was manned until 1986. The cape is also home to a large seal colony which can be viewed from a close proximity.

Bottom:
Oriental Bay, a Wellington city beach. The sand in this bay does not hail from here but from ballast discarded by sailing boats.

Miramar Peninsula was originally an island and was connected to the mainland by seismic activity. Today it is the largest flat area in Wellington which is why the international airport is located there. The bays and beaches are popular local haunts for water sporting activities

Top left:
Kau Bay.

Above:
Mahanga Bay.

Above:
Scarching Bay.

Above:
Karaka Bay.

Above:
Worser Bay.

Above:
Breaker Bay.

Above:
Lyall Bay.

Above:
Houghton Bay.

The southern part of the Golden Coast, i.e., the coast between Foxton and Paekakariki, is referred to as the Kapiti Coast. The popular holiday and recreational area features numerous parks and natural reserves and a range of beautiful beaches with fine white sand good for swimming and water sports.

Left:
Pukerua Bay, a bay by the like-named suburb of Porirua City.

Left:
Paraparaumu Beach lies sheltered on the windward side of Kapiti Island and for that reason is particularly popular not just with the locals.

Left and below:
Te Horo Beach and Otaki Beach are swimming beaches with townships of the same names a little further inland.

Above:
10 km west of Levin is Hokio Beach which lends itself to swimming and water sports. The Hokio Beach settlement is older than Levin and was once a stopping point for Cobb & Co. coaches which used the beach as a "road" on route from Wellington to the north.

Top:
Waikanae Beach with its extended beaches and lupine-covered sand dunes offers good recreational possibilities.

Above:
Foxton Beach at the mouth of Manawatu River is an officially designated road.

Left and below:
White baiters at Himatangi Beach. The tiny fish are a national delicacy.

Double page 110/111:
Himatangi Beach. In the background are the well-known Manawatu sand dunes, part of a gigantic field of dunes which stretches 200 km from Patea to Paekakariki, measuring 18 km at its widest point.

Left:
Waiinu Beach lies some 20 km north-west of Wanganui.

Left:
Between red sandstone cliffs at Waverley Beach you find caves and crescent-shaped beaches.

Left:
The driftwood-studded beach of Wanganui draws fishermen.

The "Surf Coast" round Mt Egmont is particularly popular with surfers given the great waves.

Top:
The beach at Hawera, the southern end of the Surf Coast.

Right:
In 1844, Europeans discovered the first bones of the giant, extinct moa bird on Ohawe Beach in the South Taranaki Bight.

Right:
Kaupokonui Beach, some 4 km south-west of the like-named township offers safe swimming and fishing.

Right:
The township of Opunake refers to itself as the ‚best on the west' primarily because of its beautiful beaches.

Above and top left:
A small back road leads to this exposed beach and the Cape Egmont lighthouse located there. The lighthouse started operating on August 1, 1881 and was manned until 1986. The light is emitted from a 20 m high, white, cast iron tower 33 m above sea level.

Left, second picture from above:
Tataraimaka Pa Reserve lies on the Timaru Stream and is one of those unfortunate pieces of land over which massive land right battles were fought between the local Maori and European settlers, eventuating in the Taranaki wars.

Left:
Oakura Beach is ideal for surfing and swimming and is thus a popular holiday spot.

Left and above:
The local coast at New Plymouth.

Right:
Black iron sand and many washed up shells characterize Mokau Beach.

Right:
The fiord-like bay of Kawhia Harbour on the west coast of the North Island about half way between Auckland and New Plymouth has numerous side arms. The harbour entrance is narrow and hidden and was consequently overlooked by Captain Cook when he circumnavigated New Zealand in the year 1770.

Right and above:
The sand dunes at Ocean Beach near Kawhia.

115

On the north-western tip of New Zealand's South Island lies Cape Farewell. Farewell Spit, a narrow tapered sand bank curving gentle 35 km or so eastwards protrudes from the cape. The sand bank which is approx. 500 m wide with dunes up to 30 m high and the approx. 6 km long mud flat on the southern provide a natural reserve for numerous species of birds. You can only see them by foot or as part of a guided tour.

Above:
Golden Bay near Collingwood.

Below:
Farewell Spit.

Double page 122/123:
In the Puponga Farm park area there are idyllic beaches and interesting rock formations.

Parapara Beach on the northern foot of Parapara Ridge at Golden Bay. On the beaches here are deposits of iron sand which are no longer used industrially. According to Maori legend a Taniwha or dreadful water monster lived in Parapara Bay. A painting of the monster hangs in the Telegraph Hotel in Takaka.

Left and below:
Coastal scenery between Pohara and Tarakohe in Golden Bay. A particularly beautiful beach and an impressive coastline make Pohara a popular holiday spot.

Abel Tasman National Park covering 22,530 hectares is the smallest national park in New Zealand and lies on the headland which separates Golden Bay from Tasman Bay. Especially in the summer months it is one of the most visited national parks in New Zealand. The park's steep coastline is characterized by many bays and inlets in which a great variety of maritime life forms live – these include whales, dolphins, seals and porpoises. The mainland climbs a steep 500 m or more from the coast and on the elevated Canaan plain five rivers have their source, flowing from there down to the sea. On the coast the cliffs are attacked by wind, rain and sea and broken down into feldspar, quartz and mica, exposing their crystal structure. Crystals break off and mix with the sand creating the sparkling sands the Abel Tasman National Park is known for.

Double page 126/27:
The famous Totaranui Bay in Abel Tasman National Park is a real treat for the eye.

The city of Nelson has approx. 48,000 residents and extends along the coast of Nelson Haven, a sheltered inlet at the top end of Tasman Bay. Its situation in the lowlands, south of the bay, enclosed on all sides by hills – except in the north – accounts for a mild, steady climate making it a popular place to live. The Port of Nelson, the most important harbour in the region, is a terminal for overseas ships and offers modern systems for freight processing.

The Marlborough Sounds (starting page 129) on the north-east of New Zealand's South Island comprise a system of sea-flooded valleys and forested islands stretching between Tasman Bay in the west and Cook Strait in the east. It consists of two main arms, Pelorus and Queen Charlotte Sound as well as numerous side arms, bays, beaches islands and mountains. This unique landscape was created when large land masses sunk. The sounds were once part of the Richmond Ranges which since the Pliocene, 7.7 million years ago, has moved about 53 km forwards plunging into the sea. The reason for this land movement which still continues in a northerly direction today at the pace of about 6.6 mm per year is the location of the sounds on the border of two tectonic plates, the Indian and the Indo-Australian plates. The bedrock was formed as long as 280 million years ago. You can find sediment and volcanic rock as well as a mineral belt composed of nickel, chrome, cobalt molybdenum and manganese in close proximity. The Marlborough sounds are a popular holiday destination for campers, boaters, anglers and hikers. The labyrinth of waterways can be best explored by boat.

Above:
Okiwa Bay the south-easternmost extension of Queen Charlotte Sound.

Below:
A trip on Queen Charlotte Sound offers idyllic views such as here in Governors Bay.

Picton Harbour

Picton lies in an inlet in the Marlborough Sounds whose sheer blue-green slopes drop steeply into the very still sea. Rapid growth in ferry traffic over the years has led to channelling of the Waitohi River which opens here into the sea; its swampy delta has also been reclaimed. The small city of Picton is a popular holiday spot and lives mainly from tourists arriving from the North Island by ship, who stop off here on the way through perhaps wishing to explore the scenery of the Marlborough Sounds from Picton.

Right and middle:
Boating is the name of the game in Waikawa Bay, a southern extension of Queen Charlotte Sound, as it is in almost all of the easily accessible bays here in the Sounds.

Right and double page 132/133:
If you opt for Port Underwood Road from Picton on the way south, then Karaka Point is the last good opportunity to take in the beautiful view of Queen Charlotte Sound.

Above:
Watamango Bay, a sidearm of Port Underwood.

Double page 136/137:
Robin Hood Bay was probably named by an early settler after Robin Hood Bay in Yorkshire.

Below:
Oyster Bay translated from the Maori name, Te Tio (tio = oyster). In 1838 the HMS Pelorus under the command of John Guard called here for wood, water and repairs before she left to explore the sound which now bears her name. From 1840 until the 1880s whaling stations were located in the bay. A cottage built by John Guard's son still stands at the northern end of the bay.

Above:
Located in Kakapo Bay which is named after the dark green bird (Strigops habroptilus), was John Guard's second whaling station. As many as 150 whalers would work here on the 20 whaling schooners. Hundreds of tonnes of amber oil were drawn each year from the bay.

Below:
John Blenkinsopp – whose unreasonable trading practices eventually led to the Wairau Affray – had a whaling station here in Ocean Bay. The bay was named by early whalers for its view of the Pacific.

Page 138:
Cloudy Bay which curves from Port Underwood in a long crescent to south of Blenheim.

On the rocky south-eastern coast of the Kaikoura Peninsula resides a large seal colony with several hundred members; yellow-eyed penguins and other sea birds also reside here. Organized boat tours in the waters off the coast promise sightings of whales, dolphins and wandering albatross.

Above:
Captain Robert Fyffe, a pioneer settler from Kaikoura, built a whaling station in South Bay in 1843.

Below:
Between Goose Bay and Oaro. Goose Bay, also a small farming and fishing town at the mouth of the Ote Makura River was a Maori cultural centre prior to its European settlement and subsequently the site of a whaling station. Oaro on the Oaro River specializes in the harvesting of crayfish which can be purchased or tasted along the roadside.

Port Robinson not far from the mouth of the Hurunui River.

Motunau Beach at the mouth of the Motunau River. Numerous fossils have been found on the north side of the river mouth including those of crustaceans and sea birds which lived here 10 million years ago.

Above:
Amberley Beach is a popular holiday spot for Christchurch residents.

Below:
Woodend Beach is just 20 minutes by car north of Christchurch and as it is a good spot for camping, swimming and angling is very popular on the weekends.

Above, below and double page 144/145:

Lyttelton lies on the coastal border of the Canterbury Plains at the southern end of Pegasus Bay and at the confluence of the Avon and Heathcote Rivers. The Port Hills which rise to a height of some 500 m separate Christchurch from Lyttelton Harbour and Banks Peninsula. Lyttelton is the harbour for Christchurch and also the most important harbour in the Canterbury region Two tunnels were driven through the Port Hills, one for trains and one for road vehicles to create the shortest possible route into Christchurch city. The long narrow harbour on the north side of the Banks Peninsula is part of a deep crater which was formed about half a million years ago when a volcano erupted. Owing to erosion its size increased over time. From the entrance of the harbour in the east the well-protected estuary extends 14 km south-west to Governor's Bay and its deepest part at Head of the Bay. Port Hills which almost completely surround the harbour are the former rim of the old volcano crater.

Above:
Sumner is situated 11 km south-east of the centre of Christchurch; it can be easily reached by public transport and is thus a popular recreational spot all year round. With its safe beaches and numerous rock pools it is an ideal location for families with children.

Page 146 bottom and all pictures on this page:
Some 9 km north-east of Christchurch city centre is New Brighton with its beloved surf beach.

Double page 148/149:
The 1,165 km² Banks Peninsula, which measures 27 km across at its widest point extends approx. 48 km in an eastward direction and separates Canterbury Bay in the south from Pegasus Bay in the north. The present-day headland was originally an island distinct from the mainland, whose two peaks were blown off in a volcanic eruption about half a million years ago. The eruption caused two deep craters which over time increased in size as a result of erosion and which today form Lyttelton Harbour on the north coast and Akaroa Harbour on the south coast. The connection between the mainland and the island happened over the course of thousands of years as the layer of alluvial deposits on the coast of Canterbury formed when sediment carried by rivers from the Southern Alps reached the foot of the island. The landscape of Banks Peninsula is extremely hilly with a sharply contoured coastline.

Left:
Coast near St Andrews

Left:
Beach at Makikihi.

Left:
Penguin Beach at Oamaru, home of the Oamaru Blue Penguin Colony.

Left:
The beach at Hampden.

Double page 152/153:
The beach at Moeraki and its principal attraction – the Moeraki boulders.

Katiki Point. The beach offers has good bathing and picnicking possibilities. You can also find some smaller examples of the well-known Moeraki boulders.

It is worth visiting the wooden lighthouse on the northern end of Katiki Beach which was built in 1877. Katiki Point is a popular fishing spot and with a little luck you may also see some seals and yellow-eyed penguins. In former times there was a Maori pa, Te Raki a Hineatea, on the headland which projects into the sea beneath the lighthouse – it was erected in the middle of the 19th Century in a time of bloody tribal feuds by members of the Taoka tribe.

Karitane is a popular seaside resort situated on the south side if the mouth of the Waikouaiti River and the landward end of the Huriawa Peninsula. Karitane's two beautiful beaches on the sheltered mouth of the Waikouaiti River and on the sea coast offer opportunities for all kinds of water sport.

Stretch of coast near Puketaraki, some 20 km north of Dunedin.

Dunedin, the second largest city in the South Island of New Zealand. is like an amphitheatre around the upper end of the Otago Harbour. The Otago Harbour, a fiord-like narrow bay extends in a south-westerly direction separating the Otago Peninsula from the rest of the Dunedin district.

The 25 km or so long, hilly Otago Peninsula offers numerous sights especially for nature lovers who have the chance to view interesting and rare animal species here including Royal Albatross, various types of seal and yellow-eyed penguin.

Some of the bays, beaches and landmarks are to be seen on pages 153 to 157.

Right:
Macandrew Bay.

Right:
Dustin Bay.

Left:
Broad Bay.

Left:
Te Rauone Beach.

Left:
Portobello Beach.

Left:
Otakau Point.

Left:
Pilot Beach.

Below and right:
Taiaroa Head is the only place in the world in which Northern Royal Albatross breed on inhabited mainland. From Taiaroa Head a gravel road leads to Penguin Beach on the east coast of the Otago peninsula where you can visit the breeding sited of yellow-eyed penguin.

Right:
Blanket Bay in Port Chalmers, on the hilly headland on the northern coast of Otago Harbour. The deep sea harbour at Port Chalmers is part of the Port of Otago; here ships with deep draughts can offload their shipments and containers are handled.

Double page 156/157:
Broad Bay on the Otago Peninsula.

Left:
Molyneux Bay is an excellent surf beach.

Left:
Nugget Point projects about 11 km into the sea near Kaimataitai. A lighthouse built in 1869, one of the oldest in New Zealand, stands on a hill at its end.

Left:
Pounawea Beach at the farming and holiday community of the same name is nestled at the mouth of the Catlins River.

All pictures on this page:
A gravel road leads from Otara to Waipapa Point, a low lying headland at the eastern end of Toetoes Bay. Hidden beneath the water surface are numerous rocky reefs which extend right out into the ocean. Here on April 29, one of the biggest shipping disasters in New Zealand's history occurred. On its voyage from Port Chalmers to Bluff the SS Tararua hit a reef in thick fog, about 1 km off the coast of Waipapa Point. Of the 151 people on board, 131 drowned as the ship sank and the launched lifeboats shattered on the cliffs. Directly after the catastrophe work began on erecting a lighthouse which started operating in 1884.

Top:
View of Tiwai Point from Bluff. There is a large aluminium smelter at Tiwai Point where aluminium oxide imported from Australia is processed using energy from the Manapouri Power Station.

Left and above:
Bluff Harbour is the most important harbour in Southland and other than dealing with freight it serves as a base for commercial fishing. Oysters and other shellfish are a regional speciality here (pictured above: empty oyster shells in front of an oyster processing plant)

Page161:
Porpoise Bay, a gorgeous bay with golden sand and good conditions for swimming and surfing runs south-west of the mouth of the Waikawa Harbour. Small Hector dolphins which are threatened by extinction live in the bay and with luck you may see them on a calm day. The small neighbouring Curio Bay is famous for its "fossil forest", a petrified forest which can be seen on the coast at low tide.

Left and below:
The Riverton community is situated on the south-east coast of the Jacobs River Estuary, a wide river mouth fed by the Aparima and Pourakino Rivers and connected to the Foveaux Strait by a spillway.

Left:
Kawakaputa Bay between Wakapatu Point and Oraka Point.

Right:
Pahia in Cosy Nook Bay is popular for its handy rock fishing spots.

162

Top and below right:
Colac Bay is another popular place to visit or spend the summer holidays given its beautiful beach which is excellent for bathing and surfing. There is even a monument there dedicated to surfing.

Above and below left:
Te Waewae Bay is an elongated bay reaching from Pahia Point in the east to Sand Hill Point in the west. Whales and dolphins live in the waters off Te Waewae Bay.

Pages 164 to 167:
Milford Sound is the best known and most visited of the fiords on the south-west coast of New Zealand's South Island. The 15 km long and up to 300 m deep, narrow sound covers a glacial basin which during a number of ice ages was carved into the surrounding mountains measuring up to 1,800 m. Strictly speaking therefore it is not a sound, i.e. a flooded river valley at all, but a genuine fiord, which is a steep, narrow valley cut by ice, which was than covered by the sea when the glacier receded.

The extremely high rainfalls in the region (averaging 6,000 mm per year) has led to a situation in which the sea water in the fiord is constantly covered with a layer of rain water, 2-3 m thick. This rain water which for the most part reaches the fiord through rivers, streams and waterfalls in the surrounding area is enriched with organic matter and given its lower density, barely mixes with the sea water below. Given its intensive colouration it works as a light filter creating light conditions at a depth of 10 m which would normally be found at a depth of 70 m off the coast. This enables marine animals which are accustomed to the dark to live in the shallower water of Milford Sound.

Milford Sound is surrounded by a range of impressive mountains. The best known is the 1,692 m high Mitre Peak whose characteristic silhouette, reminiscent of a bishop's mitre, is the most photographed motif in Milford Sound. On the eastern bank opposite is the Lion (1,302 m) and further in the distance the 2,045 m Mt Pembroke. Numerous spectacular waterfalls plunge down cliff faces which loom vertically upwards on the edge of the fiord to heights of 1,200 m.

The breathtaking scenery in the Milford Sound can best be viewed from the water or from the air. Most of the boat trips offered leave from Milford Sound to the entrance of the sounds and with a little luck you may be able to observe some of the marine life which resides in the fiord such as fur seals, penguins and dolphins.

Double page 168/169 and page 170 above:
The west coast of the South Island is one of the highlights for tourists in New Zealand, with its deserted, wild romantic landscapes. A mere 35,000 or so people live along the 600 km coastline which extends west of the Southern Alps graduating from giant rain forests to breathtaking coastal scenery. Pictured here, the coast near Haast Beach with a view of the Southern Alps.

Page 170 bottom:
Bruce Bay is bordered by two headlands, Heretaniwha Head and Makawhio Point; between these lie Maori Beach and Sandy Beach where you can find beautiful white quartz stones polished smooth by water and sand.

All pictures this page:
Gillespie Beach with it s black iron sand lies about 5 km north of he mouth of the Cook River.

Above and below:

Okarito lagoon opens into the Tasman Sea at Okarito. It lies in a depression between the mouth of the Whataroa River and comprises the largest undisturbed wetland area in New Zealand in which more than 70 species of bird have their habitat. The lagoon is also the hunting ground for a colony of White Heron (Egretta alba modesta), whose strictly protected breeding ground lies at the northern end of the lagoon near the mouth of the Waitangiroto River.

Above and below:
The coast near former gold-mining town of Hokitika. On December 13, 1642 The Dutch seaman Abel Tasman anchored off the coast of Okarito south of Hokitika and in so doing was the first European to set sight of New Zealand. Captain James Cook and the Frenchman Dumont d'Urville followed a similar route along the west coast with their ships in 1769 and 1826, but not one of them made a landing. The region around what today is the township of Hokitika was first penetrated by European explorers, Thomas Brunner and Charles Heaphy.

Above and below:
The harbour town of Greymouth whose harbour facilities were designed in the 19th Century by Sir John Coode; at the entrance to the harbour the water reaches a depth of 7.5 m at high tide and an average of 6.7 m at the quays thus enabling larger ships to berth there as well. The area surrounding Greymouth has one of the highest annual rainfalls in New Zealand as the narrow strip of flat land lies on the unprotected seaward side of the Southern Alps. It was thus necessary to build massive dams to protect the city from flood waters.

Page 175 and double page 176/177:
West coast between Barrytown and Punakaiki.

Pages 178, 179 and double page 180/181:
South of Punakaiki below dolomite Point on the north side of the Punakaiki River mouth is one of the main tourist attractions of the west coast, the so-called Pancake Rocks. These unique, layered limestone structures which started forming 20-30 million years ago, do indeed look like a giant stack of pancakes. In big seas the blowholes put on a spectacular show with water forcing its way through fissures and chambers in the rock to sprout forth between the rocky towers in mighty showers. The spectacle is acoustically enhanced by the droning and roaring of waves resounding in the chambers. A short, well laid out path with numerous viewing platforms leads from the car park on the street through the pancake rocks which are severely threatened by erosion.

Pages 182 and 183 and double pages 184/185 and 186/187:
Typical west coast scenery between Punakaiki and the former gold mining centre of Charleston.

Above:
Coast near Charleston on the southern end of Nine Mile Beach, which extends from Cape Foulwind all the way past Charleston.

Page 188 top and middle:
Tauranga Bay near Cape Foulwind.

Page 188 bottom and right:
Cape Foulwind is a windblown headland on the southern end of the Karamea Bight, which is situated 4 km north of Nine Mile Beach and 10 km west of the mouth of the Buller River. North-east of Cape Foulwind a single needle-shaped rock called the Giant's Tooth projects from the sea.
Abel Tasman sighted the headland on December 15, 1642 and named it Clyppygen Hoek (Rock Point). On March 20 and 21, 1770 sudden downpours and stormy winds from all directions which tossed Captain Cook's ship the Endeavour around "in a terrible swell" led Cook to christen the cape Foulwind.

New Zealand – Bays and Beaches
© January 2006, NZ Visitor Publications Ltd.
ISBN 1-877339-15-6
All editing, layout and typesetting:
NZ Visitor Publications Ltd.
Level 27, PWC Tower, 188 Quay Street, Auckland, New Zealand
Photos:
NZ Visitor Publications Ltd., Level 27, PWC Tower, 188 Quay Street, Auckland, New
Zealand, **Helga Neubauer**: all photos except: by **Werner Weiler**: page 6, page 12/13;
page 14 all photos; page 15; page 16 bottom; page 18/19; page 20 third photo from
top; page 21 second and third photo from top; page 22/23; page 33; page 34/35;
page 36/37; page 49 all photos; page 51 all photos; page 52/53; page 60/61; page 63
all photos; page 64/65; page 66 all photos; page 68/69; page 70/71; page 73; page 109
top and middle; page 146 und 147 all photos; page 148/149; page 164/165; page 166
and 167 all photos; page 178/179. By **Wolfgang Vorbeck**: page 9 bottom; page 115 third
and fourth photo from top; page 116/117 and 118/119 all photos; page 120 all photos.
Maps:
NZ Visitor Publications Ltd.
Level 27, PWC Tower, 188 Quay Street, Auckland, New Zealand
Editorial office:
NZ Visitor Publications Ltd.
Level 27, PWC Tower, 188 Quay Street, Auckland, New Zealand
Printing:
Alpina Druck, Innsbruck, Austria

Unfortunately, no liability can be assumed by the publishing company for any
statements in this book.

This book offers many an occasion for bugs to have found their way in. We are
convinced that they will have inevitably done so and would be more than happy for
you to inform us should you spot some errors. Please contact us at:

NZ Visitor Publications Ltd.
Level 27, PWC Tower, 188 Quay Street, Auckland, New Zealand
or per e-mail at:
editor@nzpublications.com

New Zealand – Bays and Beaches
© January 2006, NZ Visitor Publications Ltd.
ISBN 1-877339-15-6
All editing, layout and typesetting:
NZ Visitor Publications Ltd.
Level 27, PWC Tower, 188 Quay Street, Auckland, New Zealand
Photos:
NZ Visitor Publications Ltd., Level 27, PWC Tower, 188 Quay Street, Auckland, New
Zealand, **Helga Neubauer**: all photos except: by **Werner Weiler**: page 6, page 12/13;
page 14 all photos; page 15; page 16 bottom; page 18/19; page 20 third photo from
top; page 21 second and third photo from top; page 22/23; page 33; page 34/35;
page 36/37; page 49 all photos; page 51 all photos; page 52/53; page 60/61; page 63
all photos; page 64/65; page 66 all photos; page 68/69; page 70/71; page 73; page 109
top and middle; page 146 und 147 all photos; page 148/149; page 164/165; page 166
and 167 all photos; page 178/179. By **Wolfgang Vorbeck**: page 9 bottom; page 115 third
and fourth photo from top; page 116/117 and 118/119 all photos; page 120 all photos.
Maps:
NZ Visitor Publications Ltd.
Level 27, PWC Tower, 188 Quay Street, Auckland, New Zealand
Editorial office:
NZ Visitor Publications Ltd.
Level 27, PWC Tower, 188 Quay Street, Auckland, New Zealand
Printing:
Alpina Druck, Innsbruck, Austria

Unfortunately, no liability can be assumed by the publishing company for any
statements in this book.

This book offers many an occasion for bugs to have found their way in. We are
convinced that they will have inevitably done so and would be more than happy for
you to inform us should you spot some errors. Please contact us at:

NZ Visitor Publications Ltd.
Level 27, PWC Tower, 188 Quay Street, Auckland, New Zealand
or per e-mail at:
editor@nzpublications.com